Amazing Animals
Chimpanzees

Please visit our web site at www.garethstevens.com
For a free catalog describing our list of high-quality books,
call 1-800-542-2595 (USA) or fax: 1-877-542-2596

Library of Congress Cataloging-in-Publication Data

Albee, Sarah.
    Chimpanzees / by Sarah Albee.
            p. cm.—(Amazing animals)
        "Originally published: Pleasantville, NY: Reader's Digest Young Families, copyright 2006."
        Includes bibliographical references and index.
        ISBN-10: 0-8368-9114-7   ISBN-13: 978-0-8368-9114-0 (lib. bdg.)
        ISBN-10: 1-4339-2118-9   ISBN-13: 978-14339-2118-6 (soft cover)
        1. Chimpanzees—Juvenile literature. I. Title.
    QL737.P96A354 2009
    599.885—dc22   2008055019

This edition first published in 2010 by
Gareth Stevens Publishing
111 East 14th Street, Suite 349
New York, NY 10003

This edition copyright © 2010 by Gareth Stevens, Inc. Original edition copyright © 2006 by Reader's Digest Young Families,
Pleasantville, NY 10570

Executive Managing Editor: Lisa M. Herrington
Senior Editor: Brian Fitzgerald
Senior Designer: Keith Plechaty

Produced by Editorial Directions, Inc.

Art Direction and Page Production: The Design Lab/Kathleen Petelinsek and Gregory Lindholm

Consultant: Robert E. Budliger (Retired), NY State Department of Environmental Conservation

Photo Credits©
Front cover: Digital Vision; title page: Digital Vision; contents page: Digital Vision; pages 6–8: Digital Vision; page 9; Brand X Pictures; pages 10–11: Digital Vision; pages 12–13: Dynamic Graphics, Inc.; pages 14–15: IT Stock; page 16: Digital Vision; page 17: Dynamic Graphics, Inc.; page 19: Brand X Pictures; page 21: Digital Vision; page 22: Digital Vision; page 23: dreamstime.com/David Liu; pages 24–25: Digital Vision; page 26: Dynamic Graphics, Inc.; page 27: Corel Corporation; pages 28–29: Digital Vision; pages 30–31: Dynamic Graphics, Inc.; page 32: IT Stock; page 33: Corel Corporation; page 34: Brand X Pictures; page 35: Digital Vision; page 37: Digital Vision; pages 38–39: Dynamic Graphics, Inc.; page 40: Brand X Pictures; page 43: Dynamic Graphics, Inc.; pages 44–45: Digital Vision; page 46: Dynamic Graphics, Inc.; back cover: Digital Vision.

Printed in the United States of America

1 2 3 4 5 6 7 8 9 14 13 12 11 10 09

Amazing Animals
Chimpanzees

By Sarah Albee

Gareth Stevens
PUBLISHING

Contents

Chapter 1

A Chimpanzee Story

Aren't Chimpanzees and Monkeys the Same?

Chimpanzees are not monkeys. One big difference is that monkeys have tails and chimps do not. Chimpanzees are members of the ape family. So are gorillas and orangutans. Monkeys have their own family.

The little chimp is so excited! She is going to meet her new baby brother. Her mother carries the tiny baby over to the little chimp. The little chimp reaches out her hand and gently pats him. One by one, the other chimpanzees in the group come to meet the new baby.

The little chimp is six years old. She has lived all her life with the same group of chimpanzees. They live in a jungle in Africa. The little chimp is still very attached to her mother. She never strays too far from her. But she also loves to play with the other young chimps in the group.

When evening comes, the little chimp climbs high into a tree. She has learned how to build her own sleeping nest. It takes just a few minutes to build a soft bed of leaves and branches. She wants to stay close to her new little brother.

No Tails

Like all other apes, chimpanzees don't have tails.

Over the next few months, the little chimp and her brother become great friends. She tickles him, pats his face, and holds his hands. She helps keep him safe up in the tall trees.

The baby chimp has already learned to understand his big sister's many faces. He knows her playful face and her scolding face. He also knows the face that warns him that danger might be near. The baby chimp understands the many different sounds his sister makes. He is a fast learner.

At first the baby chimp is scared to climb trees all by himself. His big sister shows him how. Soon he is swinging hand over hand through the branches.

Common chimpanzee

Bonobo

Two Types of Chimps

There are two kinds of chimpanzees. The common chimpanzee is larger, with a lighter-colored face. The **bonobo** is slightly smaller, with a darker face. It usually has a "center part" that goes from front to back on top of its head.

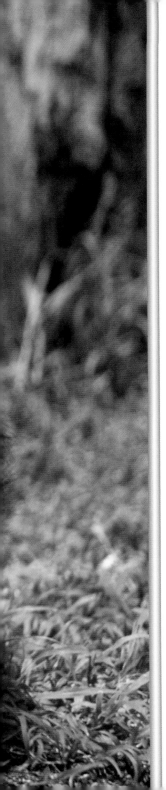

Within their large group, the little chimp introduces her brother to other chimps. They include mothers, fathers, brothers, sisters, aunts, uncles, cousins, and grandparents.

The little chimp tries to teach her brother how to stand up and take a few steps. But he won't be able to walk on his own until he is about four years old.

Both the little chimp and her mother teach the baby chimp how to find food. The mother chimp pokes a stick into a mound of dirt and pulls it out. It is covered with little insects to eat. The little chimp shows the baby chimp how to open fruit. She smashes it with a rock. Later, the little chimp and the baby chimp hear their mother's food call. It is a series of grunts, barks, and hoots. She is saying that it is time to eat.

The little chimp and baby chimp are not just brother and sister. They have become best friends, too!

Call of the Wild

Each chimpanzee has its own special hooting call.

The Body of a Chimp

Chimpanzees have good thinking skills. They know insects are probably inside this mound even though they can't see them.

One Big Family

Chimpanzees are **mammals** in a group of animals that are called **primates**. Primates also include gorillas, orangutans, monkeys, and humans. Chimpanzees are more closely related to humans than they are to any other animal.

Four features link chimpanzees and humans. First, chimpanzees and humans have more than 98 percent of the same **DNA** structure. Second, the part of the chimpanzee's brain that is used for thinking is large. Third, chimpanzees have five fingers and five toes. And fourth, the thumbs of chimpanzees are **opposable**. Humans have thumbs like these, too. These thumbs help chimps grasp and use objects.

There is a downside to being so closely related to humans. Chimps can catch many of the same diseases that people do.

Is That Me?

Chimpanzees and humans appear to be the only animals that are able to recognize themselves in a mirror.

What Chimps Look Like

Chimpanzees are smaller than humans, but they are much stronger. An adult male chimpanzee stands about 4 feet (122 centimeters) tall. But it can lift more weight than a man who is 6 feet (183 cm) tall can. Chimpanzees are covered with brown or black hair, except on their faces, ears, fingers, and toes. Their arms are very long. When a chimpanzee is born, its face is pale. As the chimp grows older, its face turns darker.

Chimpanzees have big, wide mouths. They use them to carry large items. This leaves their hands free for climbing and swinging! Chimps have big ears and sharp hearing. They also have a good sense of smell.

Smart Chimps

Chimpanzees have large brains. They can learn, solve problems, and plan ahead. They communicate with one another. This helps them share information and teach their **offspring** what they need to know. Chimpanzees make and use tools. Some chimps have even learned sign language!

Chimp School

A chimpanzee named Wash learned more than 150 wor American Sign Language. T helped her communicate w her teachers. Scientists cont try to teach chimpanzees to nize symbols for words and to communicate with huma

Like humans, no two chimpanzees look exactly alike. Each has its own unique face!

Tools and Thumbs

Years ago many scientists believed that one thing made humans unique from all other animals: the ability to make and use tools. Then a scientist named Jane Goodall spent a lot of time patiently observing chimpanzees and their behavior. One day she watched a chimp poke a stiff blade of grass into a mound of dirt. Then it put the grass into its mouth. The chimp was using the grass to "fish" for insects to eat. Animals could make tools after all!

Chimpanzees use tools for many purposes. They use leaves for drinking. And they use sticks and rocks for weapons.

Chimps' opposable thumbs help them use tools. Their thumbs are located opposite their fingers, just as humans' are. This allows chimpanzees to grasp small objects. Try picking a raisin or a penny off a table without using your thumb!

Having opposable thumbs comes in handy for grasping leaves or pulling fruit off trees.

Chimpanzees have very flexible arm joints. Chimpanzees can hang from a branch and turn almost completely around!

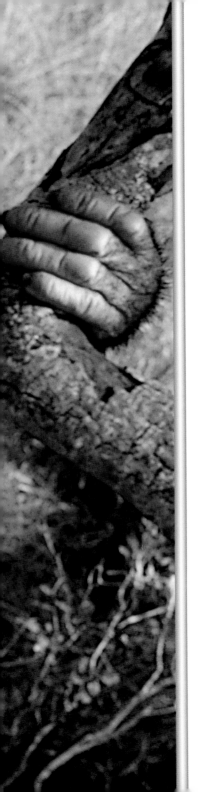

Real Swingers!

A chimpanzee's arms are very long. They are longer than its legs! A chimp uses its thumbs and big toes to grip a tree trunk with both hands and both feet as it climbs. The chimpanzee's grip and long arms make it easy to swing from tree branch to tree branch. This way of moving from place to place is called **brachiation** (bray-kee-AY-shun).

Chimps spend a lot of time in trees. But they spend up to a third of their day on the ground. Chimpanzees are **quadrupeds** (KWAHD-ruh-peds). This means they walk on the ground on all fours (two hands and two feet). They walk on the soles of their feet and on the knuckles of their hands.

Chimpanzees are able to stand up when they want to look at something. They also stand when carrying something in their hands. Sometimes they will walk on two feet for short distances. But this isn't as fast as walking on all fours!

Chapter 3
Food for Chimps

Chimpanzees can spend up to seven hours a day searching for food!

What Chimpanzees Eat

Chimpanzees' favorite food is fruit. It makes up more than half of their diet. Chimpanzees also eat leaves, flowers, honey, seeds, and bark. For a long time, people thought that chimpanzees did not eat meat. But then scientists saw chimps hunting and killing other animals, such as birds, pigs, and monkeys. Usually the **dominant** adult male in a group does the hunting. Chimpanzees also eat insects, such as ants and termites. Chimpanzees are **omnivores** (OM-nuh-vorz)—animals that eat both plants and other animals.

Most of the water that chimpanzees drink comes from fruit. Chimpanzees prepare some fruit before they eat it. The chimp chews the fruit until it forms a little ball. Then the chimpanzee dips the ball in water and sucks out the juice. Chimpanzees will also suck water from leaves. Chimps usually eat twice a day. They eat in the early morning and late afternoon.

Taste Testing

One chimpanzee will taste food first to see if it is OK before other chimps begin eating it.

Handy Tools for Eating

How do young chimpanzees learn to make and use tools to find food? They watch older chimps, especially their mothers.

To "fish" for termites or ants, a chimp squats next to a termite mound. Then it pokes a stick or stiff piece of grass into a hole. It waits for the insects to climb the "fishing pole." After a while, the chimpanzee carefully pulls the pole out. The chimp makes sure the termites aren't knocked off. Finally, it slurps them up. A chimpanzee will also use fishing tools to remove honey from beehives.

To drink water, chimpanzees crumple up leaves. Then they dip them in water and suck the water from the leaves. How do chimps get inside a hard seed or nut? They hit it with a rock. Chimps will chew the end of a twig so it fans out. This makes a perfect tool for swatting away flies!

Dr. Chimp

Scientists have discovered that chimps use plants as medicine. They treat themselves if they are sick or hurt.

Chimpanzees sometimes strip leaves off a plant stem or branch to make it more useful as a "fishing pole."

Chapter 4

Living in Groups

Chimpanzees have strong family ties with one another.

Group Living

Chimpanzees live in groups that range in size from 15 to 120 members. Usually there are smaller groups within the larger one. Sometimes a mother chimpanzee and her children form their own small group.

Each group has a dominant male chimpanzee. He is the leader. When another male challenges him, he drums on the ground with his hands and feet. He screams at the other chimp to prove he is more powerful. He may even throw sticks or rocks.

Male chimpanzees stay in their home area for their entire lives. Females often move to a new group when they are ready to start their own families.

Helping Hands

Chimpanzees clean the skin, hair, and nails of other chimps. They do this to get rid of bits of plants, soil, and insects. They also do it to bring members of the group closer together. Mother chimpanzees always groom their offspring. Chimpanzees also groom one another as a way to relax.

Chimpanzees are caring creatures. They hug and kiss one another, just like people do!

Communicating

Chimpanzees have many ways of communicating. They use different calls for different purposes. There is a food call that invites other chimps to share a meal. They use an angry screech to chase away a male chimpanzee. There is a warning call to tell the group about a **predator**. Chimps use a distance call to keep in contact with others in the group.

Different facial expressions mean different things, too. Watch out when a chimpanzee presses its lips together and is quiet. That means it is planning to attack! A smiling chimpanzee with an open mouth is showing fear or excitement.

Chimpanzees also use their bodies to communicate. A chimpanzee may want to show that it is not a threat. It will crouch, hold out its hand, or present its back. Often the more dominant chimp will calm the other by touching, kissing, and hugging it.

Loud and Clear!

Chimpanzees are noisy. They have about 30 different kinds of calls. These include howls, hoots, and screeches. Each chimp has its own special hoot. Some chimpanzee hooting calls can be heard as far as 2 miles (3.2 kilometers) away!

35

Mothers and Babies

Female chimpanzees usually have one baby at a time. The baby weighs 3 to 4 pounds (1.4 to 1.8 kilograms) at birth. For the first month of the baby's life, the mother holds her little one close and carries it everywhere she goes.

After a few weeks, the baby clings to the mother's belly with its hands and feet and is carried around upside down. After five months, the baby chimp rides on its mother's back. Chimpanzees don't learn to walk until they are four years old.

Chimpanzees have a long childhood, just as humans do. They have much to learn from their mothers, brothers, sisters, and other group members. They are taught how to build nests, communicate, and make tools. They also need to know which foods are safe to eat. Chimpanzees become adults when they reach 12 to 14 years of age.

Chimpanzee babies are usually born about five or six years apart. Older chimps usually help look after their younger siblings.

Playtime for Chimps

Young chimpanzees love to wrestle, tickle, and chase one another. Mother chimps play with their babies for hours. Many members of the chimpanzee group join in the fun and help care for the young.

Fast Weaver

In just three to five minutes, chimps can weave leaves to make a tree nest for sleeping.

Young chimps sleep with their mothers for the first several years of their lives. When night falls, chimpanzees build nests in trees for sleeping.

Chapter 5

Chimps in the World

Chimpanzees express many emotions. They swagger, shake their fists, and hug and kiss one another.

The Future of Chimps

No one is certain exactly how many chimps still live in the wild in Africa. But it is certain that the chimpanzee population is in danger.

One major reason is **habitat** loss. Chimps live in dense woodlands, rain forests, and **savannas**. These places are shrinking because of expanding human populations.

Another reason is that chimpanzees are hunted and killed by humans for food or to protect crops. Many are captured and illegally sold to zoos and medical research centers.

What Can People Do to Help?

Laws have been put in place to help protect chimpanzees from harm. But people need to follow these laws. The survival of chimpanzees depends on it.

You can help. Give your support to organizations that provide education programs and that work to protect chimpanzee habitats and populations.

Where Chimpanzees Live

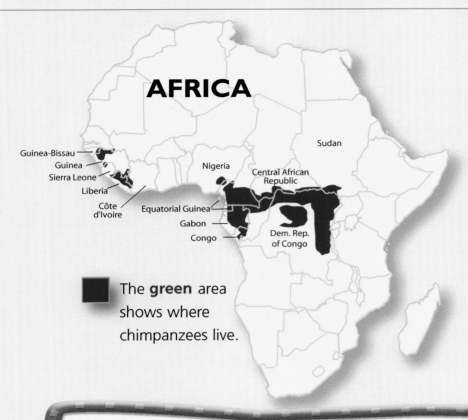

AFRICA

Guinea-Bissau
Guinea
Sierra Leone
Liberia
Côte d'Ivoire
Equatorial Guinea
Gabon
Congo
Nigeria
Central African Republic
Sudan
Dem. Rep. of Congo

The **green** area shows where chimpanzees live.

Fast Facts About Chimpanzees

Scientific name	*Pan troglodytes*
Class	Mammals
Order	Primates
Size	Standing upright, 3–4 feet (91–122 cm)
Weight	Males: 90–120 pounds (41–54 kg) Females: 60–110 pounds (27–50 kg)
Life span	Up to 45 years in the wild
Habitat	Dense woodlands, rain forests, and savannas

Glossary

bonobo—one of two kinds of chimpanzees

brachiation—a way to move by swinging with the arms from one tree branch to another

DNA—a molecule with a code that gives each living thing special characteristics

dominant—most powerful or strongest

habitat—the natural environment where an animal or plant lives

mammal—a kind of animal with a backbone and hair on its body; it drinks milk from its mother when it is born

Yes, Chimps Like Bananas!

Chimpanzees eat a lot of fruit. An adult male can eat 50 bananas at one sitting!

offspring—young animals from the same mother

omnivore—an animal that eats both plants and other animals

opposable—describing a thumb on a hand (or foot) that is opposite other fingers (or toes), allowing the animal to grasp objects

predator—an animal that hunts and eats other animals to survive

primate—a mammal with a large brain and complex hands and feet

quadruped—an animal that walks on all fours most of the time

savanna—a flat grassland area with scattered trees in a hot region of the world

Chimpanzees: Show What You Know

How much have you learned about chimpanzees? Grab a piece of paper and a pencil and write your answers down.

1. At what age does a chimp usually learn to walk?

2. What kind of chimpanzee is smaller and has a dark face?

3. At what age does a chimpanzee usually become an adult?

4. How long does it take the average chimp to make a tree nest?

5. How many different kinds of calls—hoots, screeches, and howls—do chimpanzees have?

6. What is the most common food for a chimpanzee to eat?

7. When they are swinging and climbing, how do chimps carry things?

8. What is so special about chimpanzees' thumbs?

9. Who is the leader of a chimpanzee group?

10. What dangers do chimps face today?

1. At age four 2. Bonobo 3. At age 12 to 14 4. Three to five minutes 5. About 30 6. Fruit 7. In their mouths 8. They are opposable 9. A dominant male 10. Losing their habitats and being hunted or captured by humans

For More Information

Books

Fetty, Margaret. *Chimpanzees* (Smart Animals). New York: Bearport Publishing, 2006.

Guidi, Victoria. *Who on Earth Is Jane Goodall? Champion for the Chimpanzees.* Berkeley Heights, NJ: Enslow Publishers, 2009.

Lockwood, Sophie. *Chimpanzees* (The World of Mammals). Mankato, MN: The Child's World, 2008.

Web Sites

Chimpanzee Central

www.janegoodall.org/chimp_central/default.asp

Learn about the behavior and habitats of chimpanzees, as well as Jane Goodall's work with the animals.

National Geographic Kids: Chimpanzees

http://kids.nationalgeographic.com/Animals/CreatureFeature/Chimpanzee

View photographs and videos of chimpanzees, and learn interesting facts about how they live.

Index